The Osirian Archtype

Pepi Mckenzie

Cadmus Publishing
www.cadmuspublishing.com

Published by Cadmus Publishing
www.cadmuspublishing.com

ISBN: 978-1-63751-005-6

Acknowledgements

This novel is dedicated to all of you who have abandoned me to my difficult circumstances; I survived the darkness. It's too bad you couldn't follow me into the light.

Special Honors To

My loving mother Ardella Mckenzie (R.I.P), Stacy Mckenzie, Willie (Zubby) Scott El, Jason Cheboya (R.I.P.), Adbul (Zeek) Musiqt, Willie X Lloyd Jr., Farley Cotton Sr., Calvin (Mufti) Everett, Edward (Lucky) Smith, Khabir (Pills) Rasheed, Anthony (Sugar Bear from Englewood) Edwards, John (Jon-Jon) Miles, Malachi (Manifest) Kilgore, Damion Williams (Sugar Bear from Long Beach California), Elizer Darus, Myon (Lil' skitz) Burell, Damien Jones (Sugar Bea from Long Beach, California), Ambe Mckenzie, The Mckenzie Family, Robert (Die Slow) Kendell-Bey

Dedications

This novel is dedicated to: The streets, the projects, the blocks that's hot, the trap spot, the Hoods, the Brotha's and Sista's that got knocked, the Sista's that hold down the spot when the Brotha's are on lock, those that buy back the block, those that inspired me during this period of incarceration: C-Murder, Lil Boosie, T.I., Tupac, Scarface, J Prince, Suge Knight, Meek Mill, E-40, Plies, Larry Hoover, Yo Gotti, Shyne, Trick Daddy, Suga Free, Jeff Fort, Amina Fort, Slim Thug, Young M.A., Buju Banton, Beenie Man, Kendrick Lamar, Beanie Siegal, and all the Street Nations that are uplifting Humanity, rebuilding their neighborhoods, and remaining positive - Stop The Violence.

DEDICATION

Who we are cannot be separated where we are from.

Universal Brotherhood in Statesville
Larry Hoover (top 2nd left) Mahdi (top 2nd right) Don Smokey (top 1st) Bobby
Gore (bottom center)

UNIQUE FEATURES OF THIS BOOK

The unique feature of this book is its practicality on how to shape your thoughts and future. Here, you are presented with a narrative, and ten precepts, which can apply in "your" world. The other unique feature of this book is the correlation between contemporary gang literature and ancient Kemetic philosophy. This is one of the most powerful self-improvement books ever written.

About The Author

I am Mwati Pepi Mckenzie. I hail from Minneapolis, Minnesota. Twenty-seven years ago I was convicted and sentenced to thirty-years-to-life, for the role I played in unjustly taking another human beings life.[1] That was a tragedy for which I am remorseful, and I deeply regret. Since the 42 Maat principles prohibited my actions; I am paying my price, and I will spend the rest of my days repairing the harm I have caused. Twenty-seven years of incarceration has given me time to ruminate on the forty-five years I have lived. Seventy five percent of it was pure chaos and disorder. From a dysfunctional family, to the yellow brick road, that led me to the doorsteps of my psychological destruction.

It may be grim, however, there were a multitude of hard knock lessons and growing pains that have come to be blessings. It is from those hard knock lessons and growing pains, prompted me to write this book, and the ten development and growth steps, I used to assist me in distancing myself from a gang lifestyle that contributed to my endorsing antisocial values. Although, I am not a sociologist, psychologist, Egyptologist, theologian, or theurgist. I know I have, at some point in my life, contributed to the destruction of the black community. Since I have spent a majority of my life accepting and endorsing antisocial beliefs, it is time for me to repair the harm by promoting a prosocial philosophy, which can help others during their life's journey, by presenting to them a revolutionary and positive message, which will inspire people to refocus and reach their full potential. **My mission is** *not* to promote or endorse the Vice Lord philosophy. My mission is to *teach*. I am inspiring people by speaking their sub-cultural language. Since I have the ability to speak their language, I will use their language to show them how to be better human beings. My other objective is to provide insight to the status quo, into how a gang's literature (philosophy) can refine an individual's antisocial psyche. It must be clear, I have an "anti-ignorance" philosophy, which is the central theme of this work. If we don't know the potential that lies within us we can only fail humanity. Take hold of the Kemetic knowledge in these works, and Uplift Fallen Humanity. I am no longer the hate that hate made, I am **A MAN**.

---

1 See State v. Mwati Mckenzie, 532 N.W. 2d 210 (1995).

WARNING-DISCLAIMER

This book is designed to provide information about ancient Kemetic symbols and Vice Lord symbols, and the parallel between them. It is sold with the understanding that the publisher and author are not engaged in rendering legal or other professional services. If legal or other expert assistance is required, the services of a competent professional should be sought. It is not the purpose of this book to reprint all the information that is otherwise available to authors and/or publishers, but instead to complement, amplify and supplement other texts. You are urged to read all the available material enumerated in the bibliography and learn, as much as possible, about Kemetic philosophy. The purpose of this book is to educate and inform. This book is a work of non-fiction that can be supported by either Biblical, Quranic, Hebraic criticism(s), or archeological evidence. The author shall have neither liability nor responsibility to any person or entity with respect to any loss or damage caused, or alleged to have been caused, directly or indirectly by the information contained in this book.

Why I Wrote This Book

At the outset of pondering what I wanted to write about regarding my experience as a Vice Lord, I knew I did not want to share experiences which mirror the same stories of the typical dysfunctional gang lifestyle. I strove to write something profound. Something that had never been written. Something that would inspire others to overcome their struggles, and have a better understanding of themselves. The blessing of incarceration gave me the time to study Kemetic philosophy. While studying Kemetic philosophy, I was introduced to the Osirian Tale. It was the Osirian Tale that allowed me to see the nexus between the Osirian doctrine and the Vice Lord higher-self/lower-self concept. Studying the Osirian doctrine, opened my inner eye, taught me to positively, confidently, courageously control my actions, control my thoughts, mold my character, shape my condition, my psyche, environment, destiny, and compelled me to use my love and intelligence to overcome a chaotic gang lifestyle. And to write this novel for people who may not know how to constructively shape their character, conditions, environment, or create their purpose. Here, I submit the "spark" that will refine minds, families, and communities.
IT'S KMT!

FOREWORD

The unreal never is: the real never is not. This truth indeed has been seen by those who can see the true. - Bhagavad Gita

Vice Lord, the name synonymous with Mr. Willie Lloyd Sr. Although, the name Vice Lord is equated with negative aspects of the chaos and disorder in the African-American community, that wasn't always the case. The Vice Lords were similar to other positive black organizations that showed potential to be a positive force in their communities. Michelle Alexander communicates in her book, the *New Jim Crow*. "It is the war on drugs that is the pretext that intentionally undermines any black organization from financially controlling the communities in which they reside or serve". As such, the Vice Lord's 1967 economic community development agenda was neutralized by U.S. Government Counter Intelligence Programs, led by J. Edgar Hoover of the F.B.I. I will not reiterate how, why, and when, the African-American community was undermined by the Nixon, Carter, Regan, Bush, and Clinton administrations' war on drugs and war on crime, mass incarceration, super-predator stratagems, and there, overall, criminalization of black life.[2]

Although, there is a wealth of information regarding how the federal governments utilized its resources to disrupt African-Americans from economically controlling their communities. My objective is to illustrate, show, and clarify that the Vice Lords ancient Kemetic archetype Osiris is embedded in "The Statement of Love." Also, I want to be clear that the recitation of the Statement of Love is a direct link to the Kemetic deity Osiris' moral code that will set the tone, and resurrect a peaceful philosophy, and instill psychological principles to heal the psyche. Due to the deliberate destruction and annihilation of the Kemetic culture, that gave birth to everything from mathematics to architecture, has been lost, stolen, or hidden in the back rooms of museums, only to the detriment of the current generation of so-called Nigga's.[3] Since the ingenious

2 For more information about the Nixon, Carter, Regan, Bush and Clinton administrations' war on drugs, war on crime, mass incarceration, and super-predator stratagems, read Wesley Muhammad's Understanding the Assault on the Black Man, Black Manhood and Black Masculinity.
3 In the chapter, Divine Speech, I strongly denounced the use of the word nigga. I do not subscribe to such foul language. I propose people use the term Brotha or Sista when referring to black men, women, or children. Those that believe this antisocial word is a term of endearment, I challenge you to read, in their entirety, The African Origin of Civilization by Cheik Anta Diop, World's Great Men of Color by J.A. Rogers, Narrative of the Life of Frederick Douglas by Frederick Douglass, and My Bondage and My Freedom by Frederick Douglass. When you are done reading these novels, look in the mirror, and ask yourself, "Who Am I, What Am I, Why Am I". Moreover, Carter G. Woodson expressed: "if a man can control a nigga's thinking, he does not have to worry about the nigga's actions. When a man determines what a nigga shall think, the man does not have to concern himself about what the nigga will do. If a man makes

culture is silent and has no genuine voice. A revolutionized view of the Osirian archetype, therefore, must be revived. Most learn and teach about ancient Kemet from a Eurocentric, or the opulent minorities viewpoint(s), thereby, leaning in the direction of a one-sided interpretation that has been unquestionably accepted. Here, I will severe and disrupt that notion. I will illustrate, that the vignette of Osiris, not only reveals the higher and lower self-representations of the human being, I will set the tone for a new perspective. Here, I unfold NBU-The Osirian Archetype.

---

a nigga feel that he is inferior, the man does not have to compel the nigga to accept an inferior status, for the nigga will seek inferiority status without question. If a man makes a nigga think that he is justly an outcast, the man does not have to order the nigga to the back door, the nigga will go without being told; and if there is no back door, the nigga's very nature will demand a back door." (I have replaced the word slave with the contemporary, so-called, term of endearment word, nigga).

TABLE OF CONTENTS

PROLOGUE

I t is said, the most wretched men in life have been cradled into righteousness through wrong. Who'd ever think I would take my experiences and convert them into a philosophical presentation, set them to literature, and inspire others to become restored human beings?

Peace.

"Images Are Nearer Reality Than Cold Definitions."
- Isha Schwaller De Lubicz

CHAPTER ONE
THE BEGINNING OF OSIRIS

I n ancient Kemetic mythos, Osiris is the son of Geb[i] and Nut[ii]. Osiris is also the husband-man of Isis, and the posthumous father of Horus and Anpu. Osiris is one of the oldest deities and archetypes for whom records have been found. The Kemetic name is variously transliterated Asar, Aser, Weiser, Ausare, Usiris and Osiris[iii]. Osiris is an ancient Kemetic principle that is an embodiment of the living word or moral law, that is to say, this particular type of principle governs human behavior, and is the standard of the goddess Maat who is the embodiment of order, balance, and justice. Maat also represents the manifestation of truth, as well as, the intent of the individual. Hence, the commands "speak truth and do well" and "eat of my flesh and drink of my blood" are equated with Osiris. Insight into this moral mythological character will shed light on why Osiris was considered a life/death/life-resurrection deity. Further, Osiris was also associated with Kemetic agriculture, irrigation, and the new harvest each year. One of the oldest attestations of Osiris' name is derived from allusions contained in the pyramid text (circa. 2500 B.C.). Other descriptions are known as Lord of love, Lord of silence, Lord of the perfect black, Lord of light, All father, All encompassing, All knowing, All seeing consciousness, Throne of the eye. Osiris, this symbolical and mythical personification, carriers an array of archetypal ideas, images, and details for humanity. Author Clarissa Pinkola Estes explains: "Archetype exists everywhere and yet is not seeable in the usual sense, what can be seen of it in the dark cannot necessarily be seen in the daylight."[iv]

The Osirian archetype found in mythos, images, symbols, literature, and religions is the most pervasive archetype personification and resurrection model

✦ 3 ✦

in the world.[v] The Osirian mythos is begun with a didactic story about the dual nature of Osiris. For the nexus between the story and archetype to be properly understood, story and archetype must be defined or the connection will be overlooked, the true meaning lost, thereby, making the myth a literalized version of a fairy tale. Archetype is defined as: "an original model from which others are copied".

To parallel the model from which the prototype emanates, story has to be understood in its simplest form or a person will, literally, see with their eyes and hear with their ears. Clarissa Estes describes and shows the connection between the model and the avatar in story when she writes:

"... it assists greatly if we understand stories as though we are inside them, rather than as though they are outside of us. We enter into a story through the door of inner hearing. The spoken story touches the auditory nerve, which runs across the floor of the skull into the brain stem just below the pons. There the auditory impulses are relayed upward to consciousness or else, it is said, to the soul... depending on the attitude with which one listens. Ancient dissections of the auditory nerve being divided into three or more pathways deep into the brain, they surmised that the ear was meant, therefore, to hear the mundane conversations of the world. A second pathway apprehended learning and art. And the third pathway existed so the soul itself might hear guidance and gain knowledge while hear on earth. Listen then with soul-hearing now, for that is the mission of the story".

Osiris having over one-hundred titles, sixty principle forms under the eighteenth dynasty, and many mythological and symbolical aspects. Primarily, he was both Lord of fertility because of his jet black skin, and the Lord of vegetation , because Osiris is depicted with green skin. That is to say, the ancient Kemetians considered Osiris as the Lord of transformation, life, sufferings, death, and resurrection.

There are many versions of the Osirian myth; however, I prefer my literary version, which I have compiled and organized in such a manner that as to carefully connect the informative dots, so a careful examination of the story will be consistent and in harmony with other versions.[vi]

According to the myth, Ra reigned as a king of Kemet (modern day Egypt) with his wife Nut. Ra recognized that Nut was adored by Geb. As Ra saw the intrigue, he placed a ban on her time of bearing children. Ra told his wife Nut that she would not give birth to a son at that time, in any month, or any year. Djehuti had an ingenious plan; Djehuti approached the moon-god Khonsu and offered to play a game of senet with Selene, in which a wager was some of Khonsu's moonlight, which amounted to a seventieth part of each day of the year. Djehuti defeated Khonsu until he had won five whole days.[4] As a result of Djehuti's wisdom, upon the first of the five days Nut gave birth to Osiris. When Osiris was born, a voice was heard to proclaim that the lord of the earth and savior of mankind had been born.[5] n time, Osiris became king of Kemet and devoted himself to civilian humanity by teaching irrigation technics and crop sciences, and teaching the craft of husband man; he also established a moral code and bid mankind to worship gods. Having established a peaceful and flourishing Kemet, he set out to instruct other nations of the world. During his absence, his wife ruled Kemet so well that no one could do harm to the realm of Osiris. Yet, Set (Typhon), the evil one, plotted Osiris' demise upon his return to Kemet.[6] Set plotted with seventy-two wicked men along with the Queen of Ethiopia to slay him. Set secretly got the measurements of Osiris' body and had a chest made to those measurements. Osiris was then invited to a great banquet; the chest was then brought to the banqueting hall in Osiris' presence. Everyone at the feast admired the chest and desired to own it, but it did not fit any of them. By a ruse, Osiris was induced to lie down in the chest. Set and coconspirators closed the lid, nailed it shut, poured molten lead over it to seal the cracks, and threw the chest into the Nile River.[7] This occurred on the seventeenth day of the month of Athyr,[8] when Osiris was in the twenty-eighth year of his reign. The chest floated across the sea north of Kemet (Byblos), and there it was flung by waves into a tamarisk bush, and the bush grew into a mighty tree where it became embedded in the hollow of the tree. The King of Byblos admiring the tree had it cut down and made into a pillar which supported the roof of his palace. Meanwhile, Isis (Uset) was stricken with grief and cut off a lock of her hair and put on mourning apparel. She then set out in grief to find her husband's body. In the course of her search she discovered that Osiris had been united with Nepthys, in the course of her search, she discovered that Osiris had been united with Nepthys, and that Anpu, the offspring of the union, had been exposed by Nepthys as soon as he was born. Isis tracked Osiris by the help of dogs. Soon after, she learned that the chest had been carried by sea to Byblos.

At Byblos Isis talked to the queen's royal maidens, she was then made nurse to one of the kings sons. She took care of the baby prince. Instead of suckling

---

4 In ancient Kemetic mythos, the five days are called epagomenal days.

5 This statement is exhibited in the Hymn to Ra circa 1100 BCE.

6 Kemet = Ham, Kham, Khemi, Chemi, The Black Land. From this ancient higher and lower self-philosophy derive, alchemy and chemistry.

7 The name for the Nile River is Greek in origin, a version of the Semitic nakhal, or river. The Eqgyptians called the Nile River Hep-Ur or Great Hapi. This translates to helper/life giving waters.

8 The month of Athyr is during the fall equinox – October 21st-October 30th when the sun passes through Scorpio. A certain similarity with the sequence of Halloween cannot be overlooked.

the child, she allowed him to suck her finger and each night she put him into fire to consume his mortal parts, while changing herself into a swallow and grieving her fate. The queen happened to see her son in flames and cried out, thus depriving him of his immortality. Isis then told the queen her story and begged for the pillar which supported the palaces roof. The pillar was cut open. Isis took her husband Osiris out of the chest, wrapped the pillar in fine linen and anointed it with oil, and restored the pillar and gave it back to the queen. She then transported the chest by ship to Kemet, where she opened the chest and embraced the body of her husband.[9] She then hid the chest in a secret place and returned to her son Horus (Hern) in Buto.

One day Set, while out hunting by moonlight, discovered the chest and recognized the body of Osiris. He tore it into fourteen pieces,[10] which he then scattered throughout the land. Isis then acquired a boat made of papyrus and collected the fragments of Osiris' body, except the phallus, which had been swallowed by an oxyrhunchus fish. Making a false phallus out of clay, Isis impregnated herself, which resulted in the birth of Heru. Carefully, the pieces of Osiris' body were reconstituted[11] with the help of Nepthys. Anpu then embalmed and mummified Osiris' body. Meanwhile, Heru was being encouraged to use arms secretly in the marshes of the Delta at Butos, out of reach of Set.[12] As soon as he'd grown to a man's estate, he gathered his followers and prepared himself to avenge the death of his father. The battle that occurred between Heru and Set lasted many days until Heru sought and received guidance from Djehuti. After which, the battle inclined in his favor, rendering Heru victorious. Set was taken prisoner and turned over to Isis. In Isis' sympathy for Set, she set him free. Heru became enraged, turned on his mother and tore from her head the royal diadem. Djehuti witnessed this and replaced it with a helmet in the shape of a cows head. Meanwhile, Set was driven from nome to nome, and Heru acceded to the throne of his father. There were two other struggles between Set and Heru until Djehuti became their advocate and divided Kemet between the two foes.

From an archetypal perspective, this story speaks to the mysteries of duality in man. On this point, The Jesus Mysteries expresses the same conclusion. "In Egyptian mysteries, Osiris represents the Supreme Being and was proclaimed

---

9 When Osiris was reconstituted by Isis, there were only 13 pieces. The phallus was disregarded. The myth symbolized that Osiris' phallus was the representation of his pride, which led him to enjoying the extravagant material and prideful items that were the cause of Osiris' downfall.
10 Symbolically, representing the fourteen phases of the half-moon cycle.
11 This is the central teaching in the myth of Osiris - lower self being spiritually reborn.
12 Set represents feelings of pride, conceit, egoism, vanity, transient, ephemeral, superficial, pleasure seeking, anger, greed, unrest, selfishness, self-centeredness.

heir of the world and the one God".

Robert Clark refers to this duality as the "Higher-Self and Lower-Self." Clark points out, that "the higher-self, at a personal level, is like a guardian angel, teacher, and friend (in positive form) the immortal entity to which each of us in connected ... Yet this also has two aspects, the Higher-Self as Son of God, and what I term the "Lower-Self" as son of the earth spirit/world soul". This same sentiment is echoed in the Moorish Holy Koran. "There are two selves; the higher self and the lower self. The higher self is human spirit clothed with soul, made in the form of Allah. The lower self, the carnal self, the body of desires, is a reflection of the higher self, distorted by the murky ethers of the flesh...". The dual nature(s) in this story evokes an array of images, thoughts, and ideas for those that see with the minds-eye or hear with soul hearing. Due to the miseducation and misunderstanding about ancient Kemetic ideographs, pictographs, gods and goddesses being misconstrued as paganist, polytheistic, or other misguided views, and personages. The necessity to further develop and bring the connection to the minds-eye and soul hearing, in that, it will vouch for the mythos and the not the presentation of a matter-of-fact historical reality. In substantiation of this view, Gerald Massey expressed:

"The myths are not to be explained by means of the marchen, not if you collect and compare the nursery tales of all the world. But we can explain the marchen more or less by aid of the myths, or rather the mythical representation in which we can once more recover the lost key. The Aryan folktales, for example, are by no means a faithful reflection of anything; they are refracted mythology, and the representation in mythology is not direct, not literal, but mystical. Egyptian mythology, and all it signifies, lies between the Aryan or other folktales and primitive man".[vii]

This Kemetic myth speaks to the Most-High becoming an embodiment in human form and of the human intellect, reason, and morality into the field of time and space, or god within matter.[viii] This is the concept of divine incarnation, where the Most-High willed the universe, the world and all human life into existence. Osiris is the representation in the human form of the dark vast empty regions of the inner-mind, and the essence of all things manifest, and the soul of every human being. That is to say, Osiris is the Higher-Self or the primary model thereof.[13] Sir Wallis Budge expounds on this when he states:

"He (Osiris) represented to men the idea of a man who was both God and man, and he typified to the Egyptian in all ages the being who by reason of his sufferings and death as a man could sympathize with them in their won sickness

---

13 i.e., The supreme self-generative power of integration and stabilization within the human mind.

and death. The idea of his human personality also satisfied their cravings and yearning for communion with a being who, although, he was partly divine, yet had much in common with themselves. Originally, they looked upon Osiris as a man who lived on earth as they lived, who ate and drank, who suffered a cruel death, who by help of certain gods triumphed over death, and attained unto everlasting life. But what Osiris did they could also do".

Osiris is representative of the dissolute, temporal aspect of the person struggling to reach, by effort, their original state of excellence. Conversely, this aspect of the symbolic character illustrates, there is no permanent all-encompassing, all-knowing, all-seeing, or all-consciousness. It illustrates the high-self becoming bogged down in its association or in league with the human body to experience human emotion(s) and egoistic feelings. Instead of viewing Osiris as a mere Kemetic life/death/life-resurrection deity, understand that you are the contemporary Osiris who supersedes natural boundaries regardless of racial origins or social status. "The Egyptians of every period in which they are known to us believed that Osiris was of divine origin, that he suffered death and mutilation at the hands of power of evil, that after great struggle with the power of evil he rose again, that he became henceforth the king of the underworld and judge of the dead, and that because he had conquered death the righteous also must conquer death".

Thus, use your minds-eye, become the story to look at the temporal-self through the higher mind and find the sources that the Most-High expresses himself in through billions of life forms, minds, and senses that other minds are too limited to see in the vastness of creation. The Moorish Holy Koran unfolds: "No finite mind can comprehend things infinite". Since Osiris represented the life/death/life-resurrection "nature" cycle and the inundation of the Nile River, which was the herald of new life in the land of Kemet, one must examine the ancient Kemetan's agricultural and irrigation systems to understand the Nile Rivers relationship with Osiris.

"What's Free? Free Is What Nobody Else Can Tell Us What To Be. Free Is When The T.V. Ain't Controlin What We See." - Meek Mill

CHAPTER TWO
EVOLUTION, ORIGIN, FORMS OF THE ATEF CROWN

A t the beginning of this work, I laid out the five children of Geb. Through Geb's family tree, it is understood that Osiris had four younger siblings who played critical roles in Osiris' marchen. As the first born child and son of Geb and Nut, it therefore, fell to Osiris to inherit the throne of Kemet. In assuming his role, Osiris is depicted sitting on a throne wearing an Atef Crown, that consists of a high conical head covering with plumes on either side, on top of a pair of ram's horns with a uraeus (Asp) centered. Many have sought the reasoning of why Kemetic gods and goddesses adopted crowns. I will examine and unveil the reason why a crown adorns the figure of Osiris, and the symbolism behind Osiris wearing the crown. And, show the nexus between the Atef Crown and the vice lord symbol, the top hat or cylindrical crown.

The crown, the apex, the highest point of the mind. The crown is a prominent and distinguishing feature of Osiris. There were a variety of symbolic crowns or headdresses in ancient Kemet. Of the fifty crowns and headdresses, the most prominent is the Atef Crown. Albert Churchward in Signs and Symbols of Primordial Man traces the origins of the Atef Crown to the solar mythos, which represents zodiacal light, which stems from "the start Alpha in the constellation called Clava Corona, which means the key of the crown." Churchward points out that the first to wear the Atef Crown was Atum-Ra, "the father in spirit." In the solar mythos, the priests and astronomers of ancient Kemet saw that the sun was adorned with this crown as they took note of the projections in the corona of the sun were similar to the feathers on either side of the Atef Crown. Symbolically, we are reminded that everything was first worked out astronomically and then depicted in earthly form. In observation of this fact, I will review the elements of the double crown to show how crowns were symbolically used, and parallel that examination to the Atef Crown to conclude my theory of the nexus between the Atef Crown and the top hat. The double crown is said to represent lower and upper Kemet. This commonly used statement by many Egyptologists and scholars must be examined. I will reconstruct the elements or raw qualities of the double crown via a geographical review of ancient Kemet's landscape.

Lower Kemet - Faiyuin Region:

The narrow fertile strips of land along the Nile River surrounded by desserts and bordered on the Mediterranean Sea. These natural borders preserved the heritage, culture and the development of a unique way of thinking, growth, and conservation of ancient Kemet. From this land of extremes diffused modern religious, political, and academic systems. This cultural phenomenon, that emerged on the northern and northeastern shores of Lake Moeris that gave birth to a phenomenal agricultural society premised on basin irrigation. Although the historical significance of the Faiyum is vast, my focal point will be on the unique and symbolic under meaning that comes with Lower Kemet. The royal symbol that is determinative of this region is portrayed in the Kemetic goddess, Udjet, is characterized in the form of a cobra wearing a red crown of the lower portion of Kemet. She is symbolically portrayed as the protector of the northern territories.[ix] This particular animal or nature force was chosen because, the Egyptian king cobra, is one of a group of highly poisonous hooded snakes in the region of northeast Africa, the Uraeus is known to use its deadly fangs to bite their victims, or squirt poison at the eyes of its victim. The venom causes severe irritation and even blindness, and the bite of the Asp may cause death; more importantly, this snake will attack while guarding its eggs. This particular animal is portrayed wearing a red crown of Lower Egypt, represents the vast desert that served as a natural barrier, as the red cliffs stood as guardians on the western shore of the Nile. Here, both the nature force and the crown are two determinatives that the word protector encompasses. Lower Egypt is represented by the Asp with its hood extended in its protective position. With this shard of information, it can be concluded that the Uraeus was adopted because of its protective qualities. Lower Egypt refined the culture and practices that flowed from Nubia, or modern day Sudan into the beautiful snow-capped Rwenzori mountains between Uganda and Congo, to the first cataract of the Nile at Aswan (Ta-Resu[14x]) The Uraeus symbolically represents protecting the values, ideology, ideas, rituals, fetishes, and virtues that came along with the people, who carefully developed these qualities of life as they migrated from

---

14 These regions are traditionally known as mountains of the moon.

the interior of Africa to the northern delta region to Lake Moeris. Hence, the Udjet's[15] obligation to the culture promoted the health and happiness, or the wholesome way-of-life.[16] Thus, the Uraeus depicted with its hood extended, in its protective posture, rearing to spit its poison, symbolically ensuring the quality of valuing the welfare of others more highly than one's own self-interests. This animal, with its innate and divine maternal qualities [protector] is something that was recognized by a careful and observant eye.

Upper Kemet - Aswan Region:

The first cataract of the Nile is located at Aswan, (Ta-Mehu) the southern border of Egypt. This area's natural borders had sandstone cliffs that marched alongside the Nile, and were, at times, set back from the shore, and sometimes coming close to the river's edge. There were river terraces and areas of continued moisture that produced beautiful trees and vegetation. Lower Kemet is known for its contribution to its agricultural pursuits. Upper Kemet was populated by a semi-sedentary people who lived in tents, collected fruits and herbs, made weapons and hunted. As the culture advanced, Upper Kemet was portrayed by the goddess Nekhbet, who is personified by the vulture wearing the white crown, most commonly called the hodet, the white one, bright one which signifies guidance, one's consciousness or inner voice.[xi] A vulture is defined as: "Any various large, usu carrion eating birds characteristically having dark plumage and a featherless head and neck."[17] The people of this region had a very keen and observant eye. Although, the vulture is commonly known for its attributes of eating carrion.[18] However, its nurturing qualities are often times unobserved. Nor is the vulture looked at for its maternal or motherly qualities of ardently caring and providing for its young. This specific quality was recognized, because it coincided with the development of the culture as well. When culture is spoken of in this context, I speak of the nurturing and teaching aspects of the word in Upper Egypt. Like the vulture who nurtures and provides for her young, as well as, teaches her young how to fly and hunt; the people from the interior for hundreds of years had to nurture and teach all the things that they developed over that period of time, so they could be given to different generations until the nurturing and teachings were refined in Lower Egypt, and is still extant in our modern world today.

The growth and development of the past practices, rituals, procedures and belief systems of the culture is what occurred in the Aswan region. Hence,

15 The Udjet symbolizes insight, thinking deeply, critically thinking.
16 Way = past practices, rituals, fetishes, idols and worship.
17 Here, the abbreviation "usu", meaning usually, or something that happens or occurs typically.
18 Mut eating carrion symbolically represents the detachment from corporeality, materialism, or Biblically immolating and destroying the flesh.

without doubt, the vulture, the Great Mother represents the caring for and promoting the growth and development of the Kemetic belief system(s). Thus, the
qualities of the vulture equaled, providing the values and ideals to the body politic. Here, both crowns of Upper and Lower Egypt, combined, symbolize that
proverbial saying: To Protect and To Serve. The combination or unification of
these crowns, and the symbolic language was represented in the mythical character Horus, who wore the double crown, most commonly called, the shəmty.
In this combination the Shəmty Crown is representative of the "protection"
and "service" rendered to the society. Thus, ensuring that both the service (nurturing) to the culture and the protection [health, happiness, and prosperity] of
the ideals, virtue's, values will be prudently managed and ardently guarded from
any opposition to that way-of-life.

The Atef Crown - The Strength of Mind

The Atef Crown consists of a high conical head covering with plumes on
either side, on top of a pair of ram's horns and an uraeus wound around the
horns with its hood extended rearing up in a striking position.[19] Generally, a
crown is a circular ornament worn around the head as a symbol of authority,
merit, or distinction. The term is often used for a monarch or nomarch, in his
or her official capacity, as well as a monarch's rule, position, power or empire.
Simply, the crown is a symbol of the highest and denotes rank or position.
The Atef Crown is dissimilar. The feathered white crown of the Kemetic deity
Osiris, its combination of the Hadet Crown of Upper Egypt with a plume or
red ostrich feathers, speaks to much more than rank or position.

The Hadet - The Center:

The center of the crown (tall bulbous white piece), the central element of
the key to unlocking the esoteric meaning of the Atef Crown. The center of
something is essentially, a point or part of something between two extremes
that occurs or lies at an equal distance from those extremes. Here, we speak to
the balance, equanimity, these words denote that the center of the Atef Crown
represents awareness or being conscious of one's ability to control, influence,
or direct the mental chaos that resides in the psyche. These mental disorders
would be considered adverse emotional intensities, addictions, or obsessions
that adversely control, influence, or direct a person's ability to function in the
parameters of the normal composed mind. The controlling and directing of the
mind or overcoming mental deficiencies equate to the resurgence aspect of the

19 The cobra depicted with its hood extended, rearing up in striking position at the front of
the Atef Crown symbolically speaks to the protective powers of the snake. As the Atef Crown
represents the values, ideology, philosophy and obligations [protection and service] to the body
politic, by promoting health and happiness - The cobra's fire spitting powers of light protects
the quality of altruism, and selflessness.

Osirian story - that is to say, recollecting those lost qualities. Thus, the "power" to rule, direct and control the fragmented mind is the essence of the center of the Atef Crown.

The Right Plume - Morality:

The right plume represents the moral and ethical essence of a person. The spiritual, immortal or incorruptible element in a person is the strongest quality an individual can possess. It is the guardian guide and vanguard of those innate qualities that came along with us at birth. Thus, the right plume in its entire splendor is determinative of a person's moral, ethical, just and fairness qualities they possess.

The Left Plume - The Underworld:

The left plume represents the temporal qualities that are adopted by way of environmental and or physical influences. This other extreme consists because it is of a material nature. The left plume sits as a reminder for people to restrain those hubris thoughts and control their ego. Hence, the purpose and intent of the plumes on either side of the Atef Crown are for a person to understand that they are objects or details, that invoke a purpose or intent to act, and to achieve a certain result by understanding that the symbolism and adherence to certain moral standards, or qualities are for one to measure and test their proficiency in balancing the temporal and psychological selves. A person's ability to control and direct/redirect certain vices (Sat-un) while balancing the temporal and psychological selves is an essential tool that must be developed in the workshop of the mind.[20]

The Top Hat - The Cylindrical Crown:

The top hat, the cylindrical crown, the symbol the Vice Lords employs to exemplify its cause. Many may doubt the nexus between the Atef Crown and the top hat. The definitions attached hereto, nevertheless, will demonstrate the connection. The Moorish Holy Koran teaches: There are no strange happenings. The Vice Lords use the top hat as a symbol that denotes *shelter*. I shall evaluate the proposition of the word "shelter" and follow its synonymous trail. Shelter[21] is defined as: to support or maintain, justify, guard: Being, or not being, alert and watchful. With this information, the symbolism denotes that the top hat represents a person's ability in exercising or directing those infirmities/emotional intensities, addictions or obsessions that have the tendency to control, influence, or direct the normal workings of the body or mind.[22] When we come

---

20 Workshop of the mind refers to an alchemical transformation. The mind can transform any event into divine wisdom and use it as a means to attain insight.

21 Shelter = protection = shield = cover = guard = protect = defend = shelter.

22 Malachi Kilgore, The Black K.K.K. Pp. 15 (2018). Neurologists say the left hemisphere of the brain focuses on language and mathematics. The right side of the brain focuses on artistic

to the essence of the cylindrical crown, we are mindful that protecting, guarding and defending the circumference of the mind-self, which is a noteworthy feature of the Vice Lords' organization.[23] Thus, when the Atef Crown is juxtaposed with the cylindrical crown, it cannot be doubted, the silhouettes of both crowns are correlated. And, that the objectives of both crowns are analogous.

---

activities. The prefrontal cortex controls decision making and aggression ... This is why the adult human body has 206 bones; with our skulls having 28; and 8 of those 28 bones are the strongest bones in our body. Why? Because these 8 bones protect the BEST part of our part: Our Brain!

23 An example of protecting the mind-self is through reciting the Al-Fatihah to open the weekly meetings. Through reciting the Al-Fatihah, the principle of fortitude and the strength of mind that allows one to endure adversity or a balance of mind. Thee do we worship [veneration of ideals]. And thine aid we seek, show us the straightway [fortitude] is an example. The philosophy of Lordism, thus, speaks to psychological wellbeing as a means of striving to balance the mind.

"Many are called but few are chosen." - Matthew 20 verse 10

CHAPTER THREE
EVOLUTION, ORIGINS, FORMS OF THE CROOK
STAFF

T he crook-staff, while being labeled the symbol of God's authority, was an earlier Kemetic symbol. Before it was recognized as a Kemetic symbol, it was introduced to the world in Twenty-third Psalm - "They rod and thy staff comfort me".

Kemetic priests carried rods/crooks-staffs, which have been literally, and generally, interpreted as symbols of divine power or authority. Robert Clarke expounds on this point saying:

"The rod of God" was the symbol of the true prophet, of one who had God's authority, probably because he had brought forth the Higher Self; at least, this was its original meaning. The crook is an extension of it, and we can see associations with pharaoh's crook (the kheka, or the shortened form, hek) which pharaoh always carried on ceremonial occasions as a symbol of his divine power".

The associations with the crook-staff, or rod in antiquity, also has an abstract quality. The attributes, origins, forms, and history of the crook-staff roots began in ancient Kemet, and have since diffused to all parts of the world; most notably, in the Catholic Church. The forms and true meanings of the crook -staff, after its diffusion from Ancient Kemet, have changed. It is associated with the Shepard's crook - The crook affinity with the rod or lituus was also used by the Romans augurs in their divinations. Other traces of the crook-staff are the crosier - pastoral staff, or ecclesiastical ornament, as adaptation of the walking stick, which was used for support on expeditions. Most importantly, the crook staff is associated with its liturgical usage, which dates back to the fifth century (circa 432) because it was employed by bishops, dioceses, and prelates to exercise pontifical functions.[24] The most prominent form and development of the crook has been a shepherd's multi-purpose tool-of-trade to herd sheep, its religious symbol for high ranking clergy in demonstrating their responsibility for their congregation is less observed in contemporary times. This ornament was used as a weapon for defending against flock predators or offense in catching ewes or lambs therein promoting the general welfare of the flock, both, literally and metaphorically. The three early forms of the crook will further assist in understanding the symbolism of this object/emblem.

The first form was a rod bent or crooked at the top and pointed at the lower end.[25] The second was a knob, which was often surmounted by a cross called the ferula or cambuta that was sometimes borne by Popes. The third form, the top consisted of a crux decussate (Greek T), the arms being often twisted to represent two serpents opposed. This is known as the crocia, which was borne by Abbotts and Bishops of the eastern rite. Most authorities or scholars define the symbolism of crook-staff, crosier, rod, or pastoral staff as authority or jurisdiction. This was probably because early on in history, the crook-staff was presented to a Bishop which signified their authority to correct vices, stimulate piety, administer punishment, and govern with a gentleness that is moderated with sternness.

Similarly, other authorities have pointed out: "... the rod of Moses was the seal and emblem of his divine commission as well as the instrument of the miracles he wrought, so is the episcopal staff the symbol of that doctrinal and disciplinary power of bishops in virtue of they may sustain the weak faltering, confirm the wavering in faith, and lead back to the erring ones into the fold".[2627] The contemporary form of the crook consists of a middle that is straight to signify righteous rule, while the head is bent or crooked in order to draw in and attract souls to the ways of God. Therein the idea of authority and jurisdiction is again established.[xii] The true genesis of the crook is a symbol associated with ancient Kemetic deity Osiris. Most depictions of Osiris have him mummified sitting under a dias, holding in his hands the flail,[28] the Was/Set headed scepter, and the crook and wearing the Atef Crown. The idea of the crooks associations, such as shepherd tools or ecclesiastical references, are misleading, mis-

---

24 Shepard Kings are the Hyksos, Bedouins, Horites, and Hurrians who came from the Southern parts of the Caucasus Mountain range.

25 This is the oldest form - The pendum.

26 The Kemetic name Moses was given to all candidates at their baptism, and meant *saved by water*.

27 Authority unknown.

28 The flail represents detachment from one's pride and/or ego.

construed, and vague. If the crooks true purpose and abstract qualities are not propounded upon or considered, the misunderstanding of the crook and its contemporary definition makes it very difficult to see the connection between the crook and its archetype, the cane. The below definitions will further aid in developing the proper conclusion.

• **Stick:** A relatively short slender piece of wood for use as a support or firewood; a cane.

• **Staff:** A stick or pole used as a weapon or support or measuring stick; or as a symbol of authority.

• **Crook:** A hooked stick or staff that is used by a shepherd; something bent or curved.

• **Cane:** A wooden stick or metal rod carried when walking especially as added support.

These definitions show that the crook rather seems more like a cane - The definitions of authority jurisdiction, or ecclesiastical used, is not conclusive. It rather seems more like the crooks meaning is support, strength, power.[xiii] Surprisingly, the Vice Lords define their symbol, the cane, as their strength. Obviously, the shard of archetype can carry the image of the whole.

The cane is clearly, in its contemporary form, the Kemetic heqa held by Osiris.[29] Here, the fourteen attributes of Osiris must be recalled, as the three qualities of the crook are linked to the synonyms of the thirteen higher self attributes. In concert, the Moorish Holy Koran imparts a parable that tools should remind us that they are for use in the workshop of the mind where we build up the proper: character, conduct, righteousness, truth, faith, hope, love, and purity until we reach the pinnacle of life that is spent building the temple of perfected man.[30] Now that the under meaning of the heqa has been revealed, the common shape of the crook takes on an entirely different meaning and connotation. The heqa held by Osiris points to controlling and perfecting our character, conduct actions, ethics, and ridding our minds of the destructive thought patterns. Hence, the cane and its symbolic use derived from the Osirian vignette, and the messages those symbols embody, link us back to our religion;[31] our heritage, habits, culture, state of manners, methods, ways and means of doing what's right. Our ancient past is where we gain our strength, courage, and wisdom. The heqa must be given deference as it is one of the keys to a positive way-of-life, ideals, and ideology. The heqa is not just an ideographic

29 Guidance = strength = power = positive energy = divine authority (proper discernment) = control of the mind-self = fortitude.

30 Perfected man refers to being psychologically, spiritually, and physically whole.

31 Religion - Re = Back, Ligion = to hold, to link, to bind. Religion represents the common ideal of self-abnegation.

presentation of the higher- self conduct paradigm, it is a model derived from our ancient Kemetic ancestors who are the forbearers of our African ideology, ideas and ideals of morality, providence, prudence, temperance, liberality, and equity and righteousness. Our beacon of light derives from an ancient African culture, not the American dreams of narcissism, hedonism, and materialism. Thus, we must cede to the ancient African ideology and venerate our idols: Harriet Tubman, Marcus Garvey, Noble Drew Ali, Martin Luther King, Malcolm X, Yaa Asantewaa, Queen Nzinga, Ida B. Wells, Dick Gregory and Imhotep, and rid our minds of the dysfunctional American way of greed, lust, lewdness, and slander, and live and be beneficial to humanity. We must get back to venerating our mothers and fathers, respecting our elders, recognizing the great works and assortment of viewpoints by past generations, that are embedded in agriculture, irrigation technics, astronomy, history, grammar, mathematics, astrology, jurisprudence, and medicine. And use that past knowledge for subsequent generations that will emulate a Djehuti likeness [knowledge and understanding], and be an embodiment of the Maat principles, thereby becoming psychologically and ethically the highest conception of physical and moral law.[32] This state of being allows us to make more enlightened decisions, and to take truer actions, which yields positive results. Challenge your ethics, take full control of your character, conduct, thoughts, and stop committing sins against humanity.[33] To prevent committing sins against yourself and humanity, a full and complete investigation must be done to properly understand the ancestral allegories. The words and symbols are of a hidden nature, and can be made plain by studying the under-meaning. Deconstruct the Eurocentric interpretation given, research and ponder on the under-meaning. The key to understanding the crook and canes meaning, is to recognize something so obvious it can be easily overlooked. As the motif Moses was trained in all the wisdom [culture, symbols, and allegories] of Kemet, we too, must have the same objective. That is to say, study and research the ideas, the sign language, and symbols, of our ancient Kemetic past. Gerald Massey further tells us:

Sign language includes gesture signs by which the mysteries were danced or otherwise dramatized in Africa by the Pygmies (Twa People) and Bushmen;

---

32 In ancient Kemetic mythology, Maat is the daughter of Ra. She represents harmony, correctness, truth, peace, and justice. These few principles were the cornerstone of ancient Kemetic social constructs, relationships, and communities. In understanding Maat or the Maat philosophy, we must first "know" that Maat is not an external deity, entity, or some mystery that lies in the sky and is unobtainable. Maat is the disposition that has a detailed and prescribed "course" of procedures that lie within us. As in the hymn to Ra, "...Maat have written down thy "course" for thee everyday ..." With this shard of information, we have to understand the methods and procedures that have been prescribed.

33 Sin = ignorance, absence of wisdom, weak willed, foolishness.

in totemism, in fetishism, and in hieroglyphic symbols ... It is by means of sign-language that the Egyptian wisdom between words and things, also between sounds and words, in a very primitive range of human thought. (Emphasis authors).

It is by way of our ancient Kemetic thought that we learn to read and understand the sign-language that will connect us to the ideas, ideals, idols, and fetishes for proper use. When we think of the ancient Kemetic past, think in terms of "all things" that contemporarily exist began there.[34] Once that objective is at the forefront of our minds, we will begin to build and not destroy. In ancient Kemet lies the history, origins, and forms which we must return if we want to find the allegorical and metaphorical keys to our way-of-life, religion, totems, and philosophy, which is a much more higher and moral type than most suppose the cane represents. The chaotic thought of restoring the contemporary C.O.I.N.T.E.L.P.R.O policies and procedures, war on drug agendas, dilapidated school systems, ineffectual judicial systems, government welfare programs, corrupted corrections institutions, dilapidated housing projects to curtail our searching; and discovering what our ancient past will reveal, is an obstacle that must be overcome. There can be no more reasons, excuses, or justifications to do harm to ourselves [self-abnegation], community, mother and elders, or humanity (selfless service). The knowledge, understanding, and wisdom of the ancient primordial past, is one of the many keys to unlocking the circumscribed boundaries of our minds, to be the "living" name of the totemic family that the ancients left for our discovery in the vignette of Osiris, the virtuoso.

---

34 The signs and symbols, language, sounds and words, agriculture, irrigation technics, religion, mathematics, and astronomy.

CHAPTER FOUR
THE CHANNELING OF TURBULENT WATERS

griculture and irrigation is defined as:
Agriculture: the science of practice of cultivating land on a large scale.
Irrigation: to supply land crops with water by means of streams, channels, pipes.

To put ancient Kemetic crop sciences or agriculture into a clear perspective, we must journey into prehistory before ancient Kemet became the source of all spiritual and cultural life on earth. Kemetic agriculture began in the rain forest of east Africa's valley, where the Great Lakes gave birth to the Nile River. [xiv] This birth took place in the Ethiopian Highlands, which reaches thousands of feet above sea level into the atmosphere. As clouds floating from the Indian Ocean are intercepted by these mountains as they travel northward. This causes the clouds to release their life nourishing waters. The release of these waters result in a ten month rainy season (the monsoon rains), which cause Lake Tana to overflow into the Blue Nile. The Blue Nile and the Atbara River merge with the White Nile forming the Nile River. As these turbulent waters merge, they bring fertile mud and rich black silt from the Ethiopian Highlands, which in turn, bring rich top soil to the low lands enabling farmers to sow their seed in this fertile land to produce their crops using the solar energy delivered by the sun's rays. This produced an abundant amount of emmer for bread and barley for beer, chick peas, lentils, pomegranates, onions, barley, com, wheat, fruits and vegetables. The Nile Rivers mineral rich waters, not only gave life to the farmers crops, it also gave birth to human migration.[35] It is from this great lakes

35 Normandi Ellis, Imagining the World into Existence, P. 267 (2012). Egypt is [also] the seed of every other religion that grew out of the region. It can be found in the Jewish and Christian, [ancient Kushitic religion called Islam] spiritual traditions, in the hermetic traditions of old

region, traditionally known as the Rwenzori Mountains between Uganda and the Democratic Republic of Congo that human kind originated and populated the planet.[xv] As people descended from the Ethiopian Highlands to the lower Nile Valley establishing villages and communities to carry out projects for their benefit and advancement, which in turn evolved into crops fields, nomes, and independent kingdoms forming the northern and southern parts of the Nile Valley.

With this expansion and fertile Nile Valley, the Nile's narrowness necessitated adaptation and required the development of expertise in irrigation or hydraulic tecnics - precision calculations to predict the inundations of the Nile River. One way of controlling the turbulent waters of the Nile River in order to ensure economic and social benefits is explained by Leon Dixon in the *Osirian Legends* which supports the proposition that the ancient Kemtans controlled and channeled the Nile waters.

"An example of this was the invention of geometry, which was necessary in order to delimit property after the boundary lines were obliterated by the floods… The irrigation necessary to prepare the land for crops and to ensure that the water was spread to maximum advantage over as wide an area as possible … River banks had to be cut to divert water into barren areas so that they could be brought into cultivation … As soon as it could be made fit for cultivation by dint of embanking and draining and irrigating, this stretch of earth repeatedly renewed the Nile silt, offered a wider area, a more productive soil, and a more favorable habitat for the growth of a prolific race than the narrow, or rather much narrower, valley of upper Egypt."

The science of channeling and controlling the Nile River produced thirty-six thousand years of pharaonic reigns and thirty dynasties, which represented three hundred and thirty pharaohs.[36] Even with this fantastic feat, it was the "inundation" of the Nile River that created its value to mankind. It was the understanding of the Nile Rivers inundation and irrigation process that spawned the idea of man associating the attributes of flora and fauna, plants and animals, which possessed these gifted aspects, were used as symbolic representations of likeness. Bauval and Brophy highlight this likeness when they describe the annual rising of the Nile River:

"In ancient (Kemet) the annual reappearance of Sirius fell close to the summer

---

Europe and of the early Americas, and even in the philosophical Greek underpinnings of our American culture (Emphasis authors).
36 Even with the perfection of the irrigation process described there is still over thirty-six thousand years of pre-dynastic history and thought that led up to this process, which starts around circa 7500 B.C. The thirty-six thousand year historical span is corroborated by ancient Kemetic astronomical records which go back at least 50,000 years to the reckoning of the Kemetic great year and the great month cycles, which takes approximately 26,000 years to complete its revolution.

solstice and coincided with the time of the Nile's inundation. Isis, as Sirius, was the "mistress of the beginning," for the Kemetic New Year was set by this event (July 19th). The New Year's ceremony texts at Dendera say Isis coaxed out the Nile and caused it to swell. The metaphor is astronomical, hydraulic, and sexual, and it parallels the function of the Isis in the myth. Sirius revives the Nile just as Isis revives Osiris. Her time of hiding from Set is when Sirius is gone from the night sky. She gives birth to her son Horus, as Sirius gives birth to the New Year, and in texts Horus and the New Year are equated. She is the vehicle for renewal of life and order. Shining for a moment, one morning in summer, she stimulates the Nile and starts the years" (Emphasis authors).

The ancient Egyptians, in irrigating crops, dug channels and cut banks to guide the turbulent waters (excess) into barren depressions (deficiency) to collect and hold the turbulent fertile waters. When the Nile River subsided, the fertile top soil left behind was collected and used to fertilize the crop fields (moderation). This crop science process was equated with Osiris, the golden grain. To better understand crop science of the neteru,[37] one must think in the abstract to grasp how such principle can manifest itself via humans, or describe human behavior. Abstract is defined as: having no material existence; theoretical rather than practical. With this definition one will have to look beyond the neteru as that which sustains life, and look to what principles agriculture and hydraulic tecnics have in common with human behavior. Many would look to religious or a philosophical school of thought as guidance in governing or describing human behavior. However, those sources of information did not exist in 7500 B.C. The ancient Kemtians used what was available to them at that time to represent different modes of thought and representation, Gerald Massey said on this point:

"Primitive or Paleolithic man was too beggarly poor in possessions to dream of shaping the super human powers of nature in human likeness ... And it is precisely because the matters of the myths had not the power to animate the universe in their own likeness that we have zoomorphic mode of representation as the sign-language of totemism in mythology. On every line of research we discover that the representation of nature was preanthromorphic at first, as

---

37 Bauval and Brophy, in their work *Black Genesis* makes clear, The Kemetians saw Orion as a giant man representing the god of resurrection, Osiris. And, that Orion's belt was associated with the annual flooding of the Nile in affirming: ...we knew from our previous studies that much later the ancient Egyptians of the nearby Nile Valley paid particular attention to the summer solstice, because it was during this time of the year that the annual flooding of the Nile irrigated the land and brought sustenance to the crops. We also knew that this yearly hydraulic miracle was marked by the appearance of three prominent stars at dawn - those we call today Orion's belt.

we see on going back far enough, and on ever line of descent the zoomorphic passes ultimately into the human representation."

As they did with the animal in nature as a form of human representation, they also did with the earth, land, flora, water, Nile Valley, as well as the irrigation and agricultural processes. This examination and research directs us to the Osirian faith to introduce this abstract idea or principle neteru. The Osirian faith is an agricultural based faith, which introduced the transition from hunter-gatherer, pastoral, nomadic, and fishing societies to a society founded on agriculture which represented in Osiris, and is why he is depicted as green.[38][xvi] Combined with the abstract view, and the fact that this principle neteru, Osiris, the life force of creation, governs moral order, including the ranges of human behavior, and moral law were used as a representation of human behavior, emotion, thought, and action. It is this principle neteru that pulls together the abstract crop sciences idea, and shows how ancient crop sciences are the model of contemporary jurisprudence and moral standards.[xvii]

---

38 This is the personification of the growth and development process/rebirth and annual death of the Nile River.

"My Favorite Definition Of Religion Is 'A Misinterpretation Of Mythology'. And, The Misinterpretation Consists Of Precisely In Attributing Historical References To Symbols Which Properly Are Spiritual In Their Reference"
- Joseph Campbell

CHAPTER FIVE
NEB - THE FERTILE DEPRESSION

—————————————◦◦~~~◦◦◦—————————————

The science of the hydraulic systems began in the pre-unitary Fayium and Delta regions of ancient Kemet, where the Nile River formed Lake Moeris; The Kemetans built a twenty-seven mile long retaining wall which provided 27,000 acres of farmland. During the flood period, the Nile River provided new water for the lake. The water was carefully channeled into barren depressions, and they used matted covers and wooden slates to regulate the flow of water. The Encyclopedia of Ancient Egypt points out in this regard:
"Sluices and narrow ravines were devised for regulating irrigation, and gullies were cut into natural banks or placed in the retaining walls at various points so that the water could be stored or used as the seasons as the crops demanded."

This hydraulic system in pre-unitary times enabled the ancient Kemetans to transform and expand semiarid land into fertile crop fields after each inundation. It is this process of water being channeled into depressions that was equated with Osiris. Thus, the barren depressions, properly titled nebs, represent the attributes of Osiris. In *Signs and Symbols of Primordial Man*, Albert Churchward gives a shard of information that connects the barren depressions to the hieroglyphic ideograph, the neb. In explaining linear writings found on clay and ivory tablets in Egypt dating back to Neolithic times, he tells us:
"The reading of the two end tablets is Lord or Prince or Conductor of the Land of the South, who reigned, in one case, 97 years, and in the other, 85 years. Neb, Lord of, or Prince or Conductor of the lands of the South or 'Lord of the Nomes' would probably be the correct term found on these two tablets, and would indicate, in our opinion, that there must be five others, as from the Ritual we find that there were 'seven Lords of the Nomes,' in the very earliest

of times."

Thus, the message is twofold: 1. The Neolithic linear writings connecting man to ancient Kemet show there were Pharaohs far before the first dynasty and the concept of governing a society, or having a system of prudent management was in place far before modern man; and 2. The Kemetic hieroglyphs show that the neb means Lord of control, conducting, Lordship, prince or conductor of the lands. Albert Churchward touches on this matter further in his works, while connecting the prehistoric man with ancient Kemet as his birth place, dating from the Neolithic and Paleolithic ages. In establishing when certain hieroglyphic writings were made, we find the Kemetans were in their stellar mythos, and at that time of the first Horus.[39] There was an exodus or colonies that left Kemet going north, south, east, and west. With respect to the hieroglyphic writings Churchward enumerates:

"We quite agree with professor Sayce that the character underneath the hawk is not the cake t. It is the same as the first form or crown or diadem above badly written (or Neb, Lord of the North and South - Horus I). The uraeus has been added to those found, which we see above, and is probably the seventh king or Lord of the Nomes, which was missing when we wrote the former part of the re Ivory tablets. We are of the opinion that at this early period there were no letters but that each sign or hieroglyphic signified more than a letter - it was an ideographic."

Hieroglyphs are important because of their pure Kemetic origins as this particular ideograph, the neb, is equated with the barren depression. Osiris being Lord of the earth, vegetation, golden grain, regrowth of the crops, and yearly flooding of the Nile, is the nebs connection to Osiris. As such, the ideogram for the neb, the wicker basket, is one of Osiris' many symbolical personifications. [xviii] Again, we must take note of how the ancient Kemetans used nature, things, animals, and flora as representations of human behavior; in this instance, the neb. From this a twofold purpose can be gleaned: 1. The literal controlling or harnessing of the Nile waters that were diverted from the Nile River into barren depressions; and 2. Symbolically, Osiris was originally the personification of the Nile flood. Thus, Osiris was equated with the mysteries of the inundation.[40] The abstract idea of the neb represents harboring and controlling the hubris qualities in human beings. Gerald Massey makes the same point in his study of Kemetic mythology:

39 Amsu was Horus I, Osiris was the same, years later under a different mythos.
40 Leon Dixon in The Osirian Legend unfolds: Osiris was apparently at one time a water god or the god of some arm of the Nile. So when the overflow of the Nile was very great, it extended to the remotest parts of the boundaries of Egypt causing it to flower. This part of the legend can thus be seen as referring to this phenomenon of nature.

Egyptian mythology is the oldest in the world, and it did begin as an explanation of natural phenomena, but as representation by such primitive means as were viable at that time. It does not explain that the sun is a hawk or the moon a cat, or the solar god a crocodile. Such figures of fact belong to the symbolical mode of rendering in language of animals or zoo types. No better definition of 'myth' or mythology could be given than is conveyed by the word 'sem' in Egyptian. This signifies representation on the ground of likeness. Mythology, then, is representation on the ground of likeness; which lead to all the forms of sign-language that could ever be employed. ... It was the same here as in external nature the animals came first, and the predecessors of man a primary in sign language, mythology, and totemism. (Emphasis authors).

Mythology being a form of representation on the ground of likeness, a mode of thought and expression. Thus, we equate the neb with Osiris, who in his dual nature is also the personification of controlling, mastering, and restraining of the fickle nature in man, which is represented in the neb. Another example of how representation on the ground of likeness operates is reflected in the Kemetic adage, As Above So Below.[41] Here, we must note the harmonious cycle of the primeval waters above being paralleled with earth's harmonious nature cycle/ecosystem below. This thought provoking parallel of representation of the neb, makes clear that one has to understand how the ancient Kemetans thought. Gerald Massey makes this point in saying:

Thought is primarily a mental mode of representing things. Without true images of things, there is no trustworthy process of thought. Doubtless many blank forms may be filled in with a word as a substitute for thinking; but words are not the images of things, nor can they be the equivalent of the mental representation which we call thinking. It is the metaphysician who thinks, or thinks he thinks, in words alone - not the poet, dramatists, or natural man. The augured-eyed pheasant did not think in words but in images and colors when she painted certain spots upon the feathers of her young progeny. Thought is possible without words to the animals. Thought was possible without words to inarticulate man and the mere clickers. The faculty of thinking without words is inherent in the dumb, and it is impossible that such faculty should be extinct or not exercised by articulate man. Much thinking had been acted without words before the appearance of man upon the planet. Also by homo while as yet there were no words only cries, ejaculations, and animal sounds. The dog can think without words. To make its hidden meaning heard, how pleadingly he will beseech without one sound of human speech. So it is with human being ...

---

41 This statement is symbolized by the Nsar Nsar, or the mythological six pointed Star of David.

Thought does not need to spell its way into letters. We are thinking all the while as the process of mental representation, and do not go on words when we are not called upon to speak.

Now, that I have called upon you to not to speak, but to think in an ideographic and pictographic mode; the association of mythological symbols as a form of representation will not be lost.

"Wake Up Everybody No More Sleeping In Bed, No More Backwards Thinking, Time For Thinking Ahead" - Eight Ball

CHAPTER SIX
THE ANIMALISTIC NATURE AND THE HUMAN
REPRESENTATION

W e now look at the hieroglyphic or ideograph of the quail chick for the understanding of how animals nature was represented in the likeness of human behavior. This is exceedingly important to understanding modes of representation via Kemetic hieroglyphs. Robert Clarke points out.

The ancient Egyptians symbolized many forces and facets of the collective conscious - their "other world" - by animals, and used practically every animal known to them for the purpose.

Since modes of representation have evolved with different phases of the lunar, stellar, and solar mythos, and changed even more as they were discovered by modem man. The divine words, mythos, sign-language, and totems became Eurocentric subjective conclusions from conventional authorities; who can offer no sincere guidance concerning subjects of the primordial African, who thought in "things" and apprehended with the "physical sense" alone. The living ideographs, zootypes, and Kemetic hieroglyphs show the connection between words and things, as well as, between sounds and words; these were primary and can only be traced to the primordial. A person had to look there to come to a correct conclusion, or end up with a literalized miracle, marvel, or fable from a child's mind. The ancient Kemetans knew and understood the wisdom of ancient Kemet, and the land's explanations of its nature. Sign-language, ideographs, typhonian types, totemism, hieroglyphs, and mythology, stands firm wherever these modes survive. Due to the makers of the myths not having the ability to animate nature in their likeness, we have different forms and modes of representation. In modern fables and superstitious beliefs, for example, we have become familiar with the name of the Devil, Satan, or Lucifer, and the fairy tale image it holds. This image, however, can be traced to the ancient Kemetic mythos. The true origin of the symbolical character, according to Kemetic mythos: Set, Sut, Sat, Sat, became the opponent of Heru. Mythologically, when Heru was an infant, his father Osiris was slain by Osiris' evil brother Set. As a result, Set became the treacherous opponent of Heru. Heru eventually slayed Set. A close study of the myth, we come to find through depictions, images, and descriptions of the symbolical character Set, or other typhonian types, that Set was the Apap dragon or reptile of Africa. Gerald Massey points out.

"He (Sut) was the 'original devil' in the wilderness, the cause of drought and the creator of thirst. As the hippopotamus, Sut, like Apt the mother, was of a 'red complexion.' As the betrayer of his brother Osiris, Sut was brought on with Jesus - legend in the character of Judas, the traitor ... folklore in many lands is the final fragmentary form in which the ancient wisdom - the wisdom of old Egypt - still survives as old wives fables, parables, riddles, allegorical sayings, and superstitious beliefs, consecrated by the ignorance which has taken place of the primitive knowledge concerning the mythical mode of representation" (Emphasis authors).

It is through the fragmented forms of ancient Kemetic wisdom that, hieroglyphs and superstitious beliefs, solidified the ignorance of scholars that have taken the place of the true mythical modes of representation. Keeping mythical modes of representation in mind when viewing the hieroglyph, the quail chick, the connection of the nature force and the elemental attributes have to be equated with the animal and paralleled with the human type. Then it will be clear that the ideograph, the quail chick, is represented only in the Kemetic hieroglyph by means of the zootypes or the signs and language of the animals. Illustratively, the hieroglyph depicts a quail chick. As mentioned, the connection of the force of the element has to be paralleled with the animal, and placed side-by-side with the human type. Albert Churchward is describing signs in the language of animals briefly mentions this particular hieroglyph. In a battle between Horus and El Shadai, Churchward says:

"El is the highest being the star-god on the summit of the mount, but, after his fight with Horus, was deposed and became the type of the evil one (god of darkness and ignorance), and Horus superseded him."

Here, Horus was represented by the Kemetic hieroglyph twisted flax, the quail chick (Hu or Iu).[42] Churchward defines Hu as the Son of Ptah. He but-

42 Albert Churchward's interpretation of Hu is more in line with Iu, Son of Ptah. The combination of the twisted flax, however, added with the quail chick is in line with Hu representing self-possession of base elements. The promotion of mental, moral, or societal health, which is

tresses his conclusion in maintaining:

"Ptah was the first father god, and therefore, we have the son, Hu, Iu, Iahu and various other names for one and the same. In Eschatology Iu was Amsu-Horus, the risen, Horus "in spirit form" who had been crucified on the Tatt cross in Amenta, and risen as the glorified spirit-the son of the father-both one and the same."[43]

The Hu in Churchward's works certainly may mean "the son of the father, the son of Ptah, or the contemporary Jesus archetype. My independent examination of the chief properties of the quail chick is more in line with the base elements, or elementary state of the animal presented.[44] The quail chicks nature attributes; thus, represents, in its primitive form, ignorance, immaturity, or lack of experience. From this conclusion it can be determined that the quail chick's nature is similar to a young child who points and says: "look at the fat man mommy," while in a crowded grocery store. This is also equivalent to the untamed ego of an immature adult. Here, the force of the element is equated with the animal and paralleled with the human behavior are known as vices. Concluding, the base elements of the Hu (pronounced long o as in lose or moon) represent vices; such as the id, or super ego, or the unrestrained qualities in human beings. Gerald Massey points out:

"Unless the thinking can be done in the ideographic types of thought merely reading the hieroglyphs as phonetics is but a first lesson in sign-language."

Understanding this point. The application of this divine images/language must be understood in an ideographic thought, or true significance will be over-looked. In light of this, Churchward points out:

"Although a single name certainly does not manifest to us all the parts of a 'complex idea,' yet it must be acknowledged that in many of our 'complex ideas' the single may point to us some chief 'property' which belongs to the thing the word signifies, especially when the word or name is traced up to the original through the languages from whence it is borrowed, although it may be very precarious and uncertain, and although our words which are applied to moral and intellectual ideas will, we venture to say, be read by those who are not initiated, they will be found to signify sensible and corporeal things which cannot be misunderstood by any student seeking truth."

---

line with the Neter principle - promoting the general welfare, health, happiness and prosperity of the people.

43 Gerald Massey points out in *Ancient Egypt, The Light of the World*. In Egyptian theology Osiris is Neb-U the one and only lord.

44 Churchward's focus regarding the quail chick is the literal interpretation of the Kemetic hieroglyphic alphabet, thus, the quail chick is w, u,. When placed side-by-side and spelling the word Hu. H = twisted flax, U = quail chick, thus, we have HU = Son of Ptah.

Throughout this body of work, I have shown the chief properties of each natural element given to us by nature to study. I have given these "complex ideas" a proper understanding, in that, they may evoke from the reader an independent study of, not only themselves, but, the ancient Kemetic code. As such, the Moorish Holy Koran unfolds its chief property: Know thy Self.[45]

---

45 Hence the ancient Kemetic saying: rekh ah em a ab - I know what is in my heart is a teaching Socrates later popularized as Know Thy Self.

Pepi Mckenzie

"We Speak To Our Brother With The Best Of Speech." - Kevin Gates

CHAPTER SEVEN
MEDEW NETER - DIVINE SPEECH

⟶∘⟨⟶⟩∘⟶

The ancient Kemetans left us their records in a pictorial language or pictorial script, which they termed *medew neter*, meaning divine speech or the words of God. The pictorial script appended on commemorative inscriptions on places, coffins, temples, colleges, tombs, calcite vases, sarcophagi, and jewelry. It was after the death of Alexander the Great (323 B.C.) that the pictorial script was called hieroglyphs, whose roots come from the Greek language, hieros = sacred and gluphe or glyph = carved or carving. The medew neter was written in columns and rows, and read from left to right, left to right, or top to bottom. In reading a row you can work out which directions to read because the pictorial scripts containing humans, animals, or agricultural tools face toward the beginning of the inscription, since vowels were not present, specific signs have been identified with individual sounds. I will lay out the basics of reading and how to understand the medew neter. Once the basics are understood, your independent research and your minds-eye interpretation should complete the thought.

The Alphabet: The ancient Kemetans used a standard alphabet of twenty-four letters, each of which represented a single consonant. The sounds represented by the medew neter have been adopted from various hieroglyphic sources.[46]

Determinatives: The Kemetic scribes, in ensuring that the words conveyed the meaning intended to produce clarity, added picture signs at the end of many words. They were not generally pronounced, but were primarily to assist the

---

46 In deciphering the medew neter, you will come across what looks like the number 3. 3 is a glottal stop and is represented by the hawk. The signs transliteration sounds similar to the "throttle" of the "ah" in father, or simply "ah."

reader in determining the exact meaning of the word. The exact determinative, for example, for old is a stooping elderly man, while the determinative for festival is an alabaster basin with a diamond centered. Determinatives have a phonetic function. Picture signs, for example, for mother are represented with the vulture, the bread loaf t, and the female.

Bilateral Signs: These signs were used as shorthand. Essentially, they are signs that represent combinations of the sounds. The snake, Dj (G), combined with the hawk, ah, formed a new symbol: fire drill, dja (Ga). Such consolidation is called bilateral. The new sign for Ga is that of the fire drill. When other words use the dj sound, the fire drill symbol is still used even though there is no longer a relationship of the newer word for the fire drill. For further studies, I have attached tables of terms and names given in their commonly used forms as a guide to assist the reader in understanding other pictographs.[47]

---

47 The desert hare is an illustration of a bilateral wu connotating proliferation, increase, or multiply. This particular hieroglyph is indicative of how Vice Lords multiplied. *A Nation of Lords* by Dave Dawly, Pp. 32-33, illustrates this proliferation.

"Ignorant Ignore This The Intelligent Absorb This."
- Poor Righteous Teachers

CHAPTER EIGHT
THE AMALGAMATION OF THE MEDEW NETER

In other chapters, I laid out the basic hieroglyphs and have taken those hieroglyphs, discussed the elements and revealed their under meaning. I will amalgamate the representations to connect the dots that will make the correlations clear, so the proper essence of the Osirian archetype can be ascertained. The relationship between the neb (NB) and the hu (Hu), combined, becomes clear that Osiris is, in fact, NBU (pronounced knob boo). The significance of Osiris' ornaments (the Atef Crown and crook), the hieroglyphs, NB and the HU, and their correlation to the Vice Lords' fraternity are:

1. The Atef Crown or rams horn crown that sits upon the Kemetic deities head and its elemental qualities show, the contemporary model of the Atef Crown is the top hat;

2. The qualities and definitions of the crook show, that the contemporary model of the crook is the cane;

3. Neb, the wicker basket, and its metaphorical use as a means of restraining the turbulent waters/unrestrained emotional states of human beings, ego, or id correlates to the higher self of Osiris, or the Lord self of Osiris;

4. Hu, the quail chick and its metaphorical correlation with the unrestrained, unregulated qualities in human beings parallels itself with the lower self of Osiris, or the Vice self of Osiris. Combined: they spell Vice Lord.

The combination of the four points is a revolutionary link to ancient Kemet, which will, more than likely, be deemed unacceptable by contemporary Egyptologists or the closed world of academia and the opinions of the status quo. It is black land science that I rely on to do my studies. I am aware of how the modern world of public schools, private schools/institutions, colleges that intentionally misconstrues and misinforms, under-educates, diseducates, and miseducates the young minds about the continent that gave birth to the world's religions and technologies. This mindset has its historical root in the trans-Atlantic slave trade.[48] When the European's colonized Africa, they repressed the black mind, which allowed them to colonize information about ancient Kemet and Africa as a whole.

The reeducation of the black mind must become a necessity if we will be guided in thoughts, ideas, and spirits by a European viewpoint. There must be an Africentric/African centered philosophy which does not get caught in the traps of miseducation that is steeped in academic racism or white world supremacy agendas. This does not mean dismiss the education given and instead infers to teach yourself, and do in-depth studies of what is being taught to you. It is the minds-eye that is the key to unlocking the mysteries of ancient Kemet.[49] Those that understand the essence of the Vice Lord will see the Osirian archetype. It is my challenge to those that read these works to do their homework, study the mysteries, learn to think, and reestablish themselves in the world as international citizens. It is time to rediscover the common ground between ancient Kemet and claim the rich heritage.

---

48 This reflects how European domination and post traumatic colonialism trauma and post traumatic slavery trauma had laid roots in the minds of Black people.
49 Tupac said in his song, White Man's World: "Use your brain!"

"Love Is The Meaning Of Life, The Highpoint Of Life, It Has Dominion
Over All Lower Stages Of Mans Development And Growth"
- The Five Principles

CHAPTER NINE
TEN KEYS TO DEVELOPMENT AND GROWTH –
THE HIGH POINT OF LIFE

The revolution will not be televised the revolution will be live - Gil Scott Heron

This instruction is for those in the project hallways, those that stand on the cracked pavement of the block, those that get the real nigga blues, and those that listen to Tupac, Scarface, Boosie, and Yo Gotti, and Kevin Gates for clarity. Those that use their business savvy to make a legitimate living. Albeit, the premise of this information is about the Vice Lords heritage, however, it is a blue print for people to see and rely on the potential that lies within themselves. It is that potential that government programs were created to destroy. It is that potential that keeps true community leaders incarcerated for the entirety of their lives, or murdered for loving their communities and the residents that live in those communities. Now that the key has been handed to you, I will place it in the lock and turn it. When the door opens you will be introduced to the ten keys of development and growth. Use them to build a proper foundation to practice love, truth, peace, freedom, and justice to be a better human being.

1. Control of Thought: Take possession of your mind. Do not be misled or be swayed by adversity, obsession, or addiction. Keep your mind on the things you want and off the things you do not want.

2. The Control of Action: Do not act out of ignorance, hate, anger, or rage. Think before you do. Anything you do must be a non-negative action. Live by the Golden Rule, form a habit of tolerance.

3. Steadfastness of Purpose: Find an intellectual talent. Use your creativity: study, master and improve upon the arts of: grammar, logic, geometry, arithmetic, architecture, carpentry, plant science, pharmacology, physiology, law, astronomy, engineering, land surveying, agriculture, and politics.

4. Become like the Supreme Creator: Be an embodiment of all that is good and righteous. Access the third-eye through astral projection, deep meditation, and then build upon those ideas that have been revealed.

5. Identify with a Spiritual Life: Study and practice "any" religion. Be happy and make others happy. Be higher ideals.

6. Evidence of a mission in life: Make a mark in life, publish your thought and ideas, copyright, patent and trademark your ideas. Improve upon the liberal arts, be an inventor - Leave something behind.

7. Freedom Of Resentment When Under Persecution Or Wrong: Let the small things fly by, keep a peaceful and balanced mind, ignore the haters, give yourself positive suggestions.

8. Change Because Of Acquired Knowledge: Be that acquired knowledge, study, plan and think deeply on a daily basis.

9. Conduct Independent Study To Improve Yourself: Study your heritage, culture, history - Know Thy Self. Eliminate all negative thoughts by self-inspection.

10. Have confidence in your ability to learn and set goals.

CHAPTER TEN
WHO IS MAAT?

In previous pages, I briefly highlighted the Maat principles. In particular, I placed emphasis on the standard of the goddess Maat being the embodiment of order, balance, and justice. Maat, moreover, represents the manifestation of truth, as well as the intent of the individual. To be an embodiment of the Maat principles is essentially to be psychologically, and ethically, the highest conception of physical and moral law. In ancient Kemet, Maat principles were the cornerstone of ancient Kemetic social constructs, relationships, and communities. In understanding Maat or the Maat philosophy, we must first "know" that Maat is not an external deity, entity, or some mystery in the sky that is unobtainable. Maat is the disposition that has a detailed and prescribed "course" of procedures that lie within us.

In a hymn to Ra we find:
"The land of Manu receives thee with satisfaction, and the goddess Maat embraces thee both at morn and at eve ... the god Djehuti and the goddess Maat have written down thy daily course for thee everyday ..."

Again, Maat is a disposition that has a detailed and prescribed course of procedures that lie within us. As in the hymn, Maat has written down thy daily course for thee every day. With this shard of information, we have to understand the methods and procedures that have been prescribed. The prescribed procedures are titled *The 42 Negative Confessions*. These confessions are said to take place in the Hall of Maat where judgement is rendered after one has been mortified. Due to the ancient Kemetan's not accepting as true the concept of death as we believe it to be in contemporary times. They concluded that death represented the life/death/life-resurrection process. Decay and regeneration, thus, dictated that the 42 Negative Confessions, thereby, dictates our behavior and attitude. This indwelling divinity negates the order of thou shall not, instead, our divine innate attributes guide us in the direction of the 42 principles, which create harmony, justice, and righteousness in ourselves and in our lives. The 42 prescribed procedures are as follows:

1. I am not ignorant and I seek wisdom.
2. I do not commit robbery/I do not take from others by use of force.
3. I honor virtue
4. I do not kill or commit acts of violence/I respect human life.
5. I respect the property of others
6. I serve others selflessly.
7. I hold sacred those objects of the divine.
8. I do not lie
9. I am not greedy
10. I speak words of good intent.
11. I relate in peace.
12. I am a conservationist.
13. I can be trusted.
14. I care for the earth/I maintain a clean neighborhood.
15. I keep my own council
16. I speak positively of others.
17. I remain in balance with my emotions.
18. I am trustful in my relationships.
19. I hold purity in high esteem.
20. I spread joy.
21. I do the best I can.
22. I communicate with compassion.
23. I listen to opposing opinions.
24. I create harmony.
25. I invoke laughter.
26. I am not a person of violence.
27. I am forgiving.
28. I am non abusive/verbally abusive.
29. I do not stir up strife.
30. I am non-judgmental.
31. I follow my inner guidance.
32. I speak without disturbing others.
33. I have done no evil/I do good.
34. I give blessings/charity.

35. I keep the waters pure/never stop the thoughts of another.
36. I am humble.
37. I achieve with integrity.
38. I advance through my own abilities.
39. I embrace all/equality.
40. I have not spoken in a prideful or arrogant manner.
41. I speak with optimism.
42. I embrace the All.

These 42 declarations are the daily course that have been written down for us to practice every day. Thus, when you look in the mirror and gauge/judge your actions according to the herein prescribed principles it is you that determines to what scale you have lived in accordance with Maat. Hence, only you can judge you. When the question is posed, "Who are you?" Always answer: "I am Maat."

SELECTED BIBLIOGRAPHY

Ali Drew Noble, *Moorish Holy Koran*

Budge Wallis E.A., *The Book of the Dead* (1960)

Bauval Robert and Brophy Thomas, *Black Genesis* (2011)

Bunson Margaret, *The Encyclopedia of Ancient Egypt* (1991)

Churchward Albert, *Signs and Symbols of Primordial Man* (1993)

Clarke Robert, *Order Outside Time* (2005)

Dewey David, *A Nation of Lords* (1973)

Dixon Leon, *The Osirian Legend*

Croce Sole Maria, *Treasures of Ancient Egypt*

Freke Timothy and Gandy Peter, *Jesus Mysteries*

Massey Gerald, *Ancient Egypt The Light of the World* (1907)

Wikipedia.org, *Hieroglyphs by Common Name A-I*

Ellis Normandi, *Imagining the World into Existence* (2012)

Muhammad Wesley, *Egyptian Sacred Science and Islam* (2012)

Kilgore Malachi, *The Black K.K.K.* (2018)

NOTES

[i] Geb is the earth-god father of food; the god of fructification associated with plants, fruit, flowers, foliage. He is the lord of aliment in whom the reproduction powers of earth are ithyphallically portrayed.

[ii] The ancients apprehended that the foremost characteristic of Nut or Tefnut was its dewy moisture and refreshing coolness. The water of heaven and the tree of dawn precede this personification. The name of Tefnut, from Tef, means to drip, drop, spit, exude, shed, effuse, and supply. The name of Nut, for heaven, shows that Tefnut represented the dew or moisture that fell from there at dawn.

[iii] The proper spelling is Ausares - Aus = throne (accession to the throne), Ares = eye (observance with the eye/deference). This pronunciation and spelling is in line with Osiris' title as the All Seeing. Moreover, the Medew Neter (hieroglyphic interpretation) is as follows: Reed = I, Coiled Rope = u, Folded Cloth = s, Eye = ir, Door Bolt = s equates to, accession to the throne or observance with the eye. Moreover, in spelling Osiris' name with signifies the essence which procreates or comes into existence through abstract and concrete matter which is symbolized by the Matti goddesses: Isis and Nepthys. Thus, Osiris' name means supreme creator, supreme being, or sustainer of life; the supreme or sustainer being represented by the throne, the creator being or life by, the eye which imports awareness - Osiris is the cause of life within spiritually dead people.

[iv] Estes Pinkola Clarissa, *Women Who Run With the Wolves* Pp. 29 (1992).

[v] In substantiation of what I say regarding Osiris being "the most" pervasive archetype personification and model in the world. Timothy Freke and Peter Gandy point out: "The Egyptian myth of Osiris is the primal/myth of the mystery godman and reaches back to prehistory. The story is so ancient that it can be found in pyramid texts written over 4,500 years ago... In the same way that Osiris was synthesized by the Greeks with their indigenous god Dionysus to create the Greek mysteries, other Mediterranean deities into the dying and resurrecting mystery godman. So, the deity who was known as Osiris in Egypt and became Dionysus in Greece was called Attis in Asia Minor, Adonis in Syria, Bacchus in Italy, Mithras in Persia and so on."

[vi] Auseres is the Kemetic deity of life/death/life-resurrection. He is also associated with sprouting vegetation and the fertile flooding (life/death/life-fertility cycle) of the Nile River. This cycle is concerned with growth and development. Clarissa Estes writes: "The life/death/life nature is a cycle of animation, development, decline, death, and death is always followed by reanimation. This

cycle affects all physical life and all facets of psychological life. Everything - the sun, novas, and the moon, as well as the affairs of humans and those of the tiniest creatures, cells, and atoms alike - have this fluttering, then faltering, then fluttering again."

[vii] Dr. Charles Finch touches on this view when he writes: "Gerald Massey was a diffusionist, plain and simple. For him, the issue was unarguable: the religious ideas and symbols whose genesis is in the Nile Valley flowed outward from Africa eventually giving birth to both Judaism and Christianity. The number of parallels between those two religions on the one hand and those of the Nile Valley region on the other, are simply too abundant to admit any other conclusion... the story of Horus presages that of Moses; the epic of Osiris, the mummified and anointed kerest, prefigures that of Yahushua, the resurrected Christ. For Massey it was a Nile genesis and only through understanding the Nile genesis is the Judeo-Christian epoch intelligible."

[viii] This also speaks to the thirteen aspects of the higher-self: obedience, modesty, gratitude, charity, temperance, prudence, justice, sincerity, diligence, benevolence, science, religion, truth.

[x] The terms upper and Lower Egypt are confusing as they conflict with the way maps are read today. Lower Egypt is the north of the country. The Upper Egypt is represented by the vulture goddess Nekhbet, while Lower Egypt is represented by the Uraeus goddess Udjet.

[xi] Other terms for the Nekhbet or the vulture are:
• Mut - The Great Mother - Theopany is the vulture
• Mut - Mother
• Mu - Mother, source, life giver, bringer forth, producer,
• Ta Urt - The great Mother "earth" -The first and earliest mother
• Apt - Ta-Urt divinized

[xii] Theoretically, the arc of the crook resembles that of a crescent/half-moon. When the Nile River began its steady rise toward the flood stage, Osiris was honored declaring Osiris was found again. In honor of this waxing stage of the crescent moon to honor Osiris' return, mud and various spices were often formed into the shape of the crescent moon to honor Osiris' resurrection. The straightness of the heqa or perpendicular line stemming from the arc of the crook represents o the ability to see something form a particular viewpoint. This viewpoint speaks to a way of living, which is attributed to the goddesses Maat whose insignia, the Kharu (so-called Ankh) represents the methods, customs, and standards, that have been passed down as a way-of-life [ethical and moral principles, standards, and ideals]. Osiris is the embodiment of these ethical principles, which is why the heqa is of importance. It was carried by

those who could teach the way of living. Thus, the general terms applied are mischaracterized. Here, it is to be understood that the heqa represents Osiris' positive spirit, mind, attitude, and ethical forces that issue from the primordial womb of the Kharu.

[xiii] Heqa brings together, binds, connects and links us to the values, ways and means of our ancient Kemetic ancestor's teachings. These lessons guide and shepherd us in the proper moral and ethical direction. That is to say, the cane is an avatar of love, truth, peace, freedom, justice, sincerity, charity, humility, harmony, and understanding which are the standards which we have to live by in order to circumvent high incarceration rates, miseducation, welfare, parole, probation, child support, war on drug agendas, and all policies, laws, and acts in concert with such notions.

[xiv] The Nile River is over four thousand miles long, and is formed by the convergence of the Blue Nile and the White Nile rivers at Khartoum in the Sudan. The White Nile has its sources in two great lakes between Uganda Zaire, and the other is at the intersection of Kenya, Tanzania, and Uganda. The Blue Nile contributes approximately eighty percent of the volume of the Nile. Its source stems from another great lake, and Lake Tana located in the Ethiopian Highlands.

[xv] Wesley Muhammad, *Egyptian Sacred Science and Islam* P. 15 (2012). The entire human race outside Africa owes its existence to the survival of a single tribe of around 200 people who crossed the Red Sea 70,000 years ago, scientists have discovered ... Research by geneticists and archeologists has allowed them to trace the origins of modern homo sapiens back to a single group of people who managed to cross from the Horn of Africa and into Arabia. From there they went on to colonize the rest of the world.

[xvi] The neteru are the life forces of creation, or the life forces that sustain creation, which include: Shu (air), Neb-het (atmosphere, Nu (water), Nut (sky), Geb (earth), Ra (sun), Ausar (flora and fauna), Auset (flora fauna), Het-Heru (minerals), Set (metals),. The neteru are of three types: 1. Creator, 2. Elements, 3. Principles.

[xvii] In describing the two extremes of the narrow strips of arable land lining either bank of the Nile, from Aswan to the Northern Delta, the words in parenthesis describe this cycle of flooding and balancing the two extremes. These two extremes represents the turbulent Nile waters fertile mud and silt = black (excess), the depressions in the desert = red (deficiency), digging of depressions in the barren desert and challenging the turbulent waters into the depressions and making crop fields = green (moderation), harvesting of the crops = (reason). Thus, the controlling of the higher self and lower self, equal reasoning.

[xviii] A distinctive use of the basket hieroglyph for nb is: Lord, Master, Everything, All, Every, All Things, Lord of.

sign	how we transliterate (record) it	how we pronounce it	what it shows
	ꜣ	*a	vulture
	ỉ	*i (as in Nick)	flowering reed
	y	*y (as Y in Yasmin)	two reeds/strokes
	ꜥ	*a	forearm
	w	*w or u	quail chick
	b	*b	lower leg
	p	*p	stool
	f	*f	horned viper
	m	*m	owl / ?
	n	*n	water/crown
	r	*r	mouth
	h	*h	courtyard

sign	how we transliterate (record) it	how we pronounce it	what it shows
	ḥ	*h	twisted flax
	ḫ	*kh	jar lid
	ẖ	*kh	animal's belly
	s (the latter formerly z)	*s (*z)	cloth/door-bolt
	š	*sh	pool
	q	*k	hill slope
	k	*k.	basket
	g	*g (as in Gary)	jar stand
	t	*t	loaf/pestle
	ṯ	*tj (as Ch in Charles)	tethering rope
	d	*d	hand
	ḏ	*dj (as G in George)	cobra

Approximate pronunciation is indicated by an asterisk *. To be able to read groups of consonants, we insert short *e where necessary, so snb becomes *seneb. This is artificial; the precise pronunciation is often uncertain. Do not be confused by the fact that the suggested pronunciation of consonants ꜣ, ỉ and ꜥ, which do not occur in English, is *a, *i and *a, our vowels!

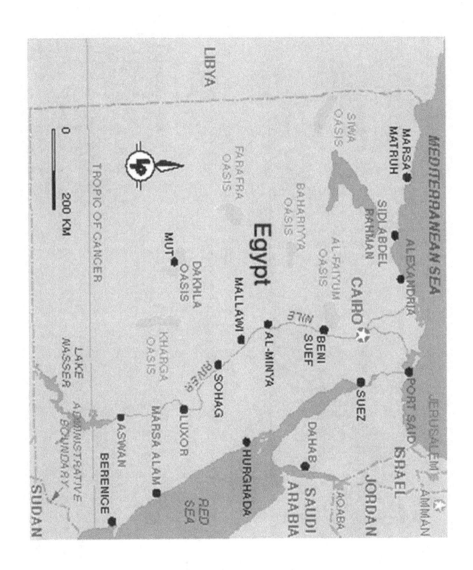

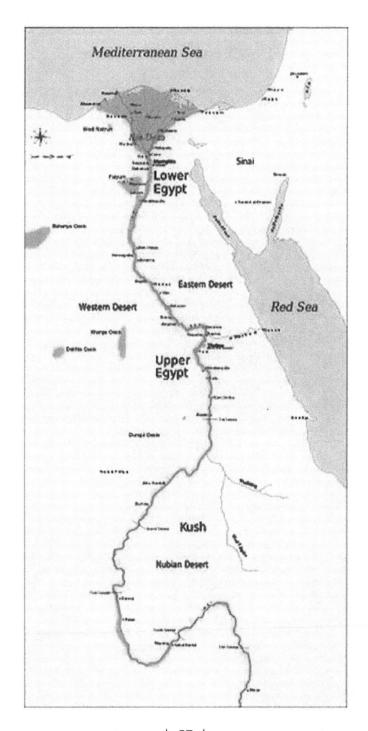

Pepi Mckenzie

One cannot serve the ideal [God] and serve one's ego, one object of worship must be put to death in order for the other to live; as one must die to the flesh to be reborn in attitude.

Pepi Mckenzie was convicted of first-degree murder in 1992. As an inactive member of the conservative Vice Lord organization, he introduces his narrative of how to heal the ghetto's ills. He has taken his hard-knock lesson acquired from pimps, hustlers, players, growing pains, prison-crats, street drama, drug dealers, and fellow gang members, and penned a revolutionized paradigm titled, NBU-The Osirian Archetype. NBU-The Osirian Archetype is aimed at transforming the agitated psyches of young adults in street gangs. Pepi Mckenzie has refined the "say no to gangs" cliché. His revolutionary and unique insight into the ancient Egyptian Osirian doctrine demonstrates the affinities and correlations between the higher/lower self-ideals. He uses the Osirian doctrine to show how an individual can transform the adversities of their psyche by applying the ten development and growth techniques. A timely look at contemporary, so called, gangs and the ancient Egyptian symbols street gangs represent is a serious study. NBU-The Osirian Archetype, offers an important and unique portrait of the Vice Lords that gave the American fraternity an understanding that gang members can become community leaders, business men and women, and the key to uplifting humanity. This body of work, this new definition, this revolutionary idea, is the paradigm that will spark a new idea.

IT'S KMT!

Who we are cannot be separated where we are from
Left- Elizer Darruis, Middle- Pepi Mckenzie, Right - Myon Burrel

CPSIA information can be obtained
at www.ICGtesting.com
Printed in the USA
BVHW041816080921
616386BV00015B/570

9 781637 510056